LULLABIES

FOR THE SOUL

Lullabies for the Soul

by

Alanya Echols

INNATE DIVINITY
San Bernardino/Houston

Copyright © 2017 by Innate Divinity Publishing

This work is protected by US copyright laws. All rights reserved. No part of this publication may be reproduced, stored in a retrieval system or transmitted in any form or by any means, electronic, mechanical, photocopying, recording or otherwise without the written permission of the publisher.
ISBN-13: 978-0-9996018-7-7 (Innate Divinity)
ISBN-10: 0999601873

Cover Design: Eric DeVaughnn

In Loving Memory:

Prance into that audition
like the queen you were

Fire in your eyes
smiling authentically

And take that role
without asking for it

anymore

©2017 Charlene E. Green
Excerpted from "Echols in the Dark"
All rights reserved.

Table of contents

In Loving Memory

Preface   1

FOR: SELF LOVE

Take Me to Heaven	5
Balance	6
Frustration	7
The Other Side of the Unknown	8
Clarity Gains	10
I Dance for Her	11
You Are Blessed	12
The Breath	13
My Plea to Society	14
Control	15

FOR: LOVE

Take Me to God	19
Him, Me, & We	20
Living Water	22
Touch	24
Express	25
From Waterfalls to Sunsets	26
Love Just Is!	28
Glide	30
Like Water	32
I've Known Him	35

In Loving Memory

The Author

Preface

Bliss-filled Words to Soothe the Spirit!

We all need soothing for our spirits, in times of sorrow, happiness, love, joy, despair, depression, anxiety, unworthiness, stress, uneasiness, indecisiveness, having to forgive, having to be forgiven, and remembering to have compassion. This book is a friendly reminder that we are becoming whole, we are a collective, we are all one in this massive universe. We are one.

These poems were written to be a song for the spirit. Whatever you need to feel, whatever you need to see, I hope you find embedded in these words. May your soul be touched, may your heart feel complete, may you be entranced with bliss and calmed by these lullabies.

Alanya Echols

FOR: SELF LOVE

Take Me to Heaven

they say there's a heaven
I say, I am ready to see

heaviness has followed
in the back of my mind for far too long
I need much more than a simple vacation

a hotel will not do
a road trip could not suffice to fill the emptiness
within my spirit

I need sunny smiles landing on my lips, daily
an aura awakened, glowing like the night I stayed up
to see the blue moon

blue…tranquility…calmness…peace…*peace*

I need the feeling of free;
like when a lover lightly brushes his fingers
on your bare shoulders

I need full body relaxation,
mind centered on wonders,
on moments that ease senses instantly

yes, take me to heaven
I am ready to go that way
this will be more than a short outing

I plan to stay
take me to heaven

Balance

balance
take me back to balance
free of attachment

peace

take me back to balance
free of attachment

I enjoy feeling free,
being at peace

take me back
ground me

settle my energy
sharpen my awareness

balance

balance

inner stability

I need

Frustration

frustration, frustration
I am wiping you away

you have no business controlling my day

yes, I am quick-witted
yes, I am slick

does not mean that anger should slip
land in the hands of someone I love

what good is lashing out?
what good is inner uneasiness?

just because my mind is not at peace
does not mean it is another's problem

if I am peace nothing can move me
if I am peace nothing can move me

instead of raising hell, I will raise myself well

by redirecting my need to control
to my need to create and cool down my inner flames

so, frustration, as you can see, this is MY day
I have chosen to indulge in pleasure

I have no time for the pain!

The Other Side…

don't become restless…

focused on negative…

what shall come …

flow with the outcome   Sometimes we sink…

we run away…

But why waste…

fearing what…

Or the other side of…

It's a part of…

Let the universe work…

Gain your mental…

and your…

regardless of…

You can shift…

accept…

let go of your control…

Freedom is on…

...of the Unknown

...or breathless

...illusions of what will

...Let go of your control

...way too deep into worry and anxiousness

...from the unknown.

...the time or energy,

...you don't know?

...the unknown?   Go...

...your growth.   to...

...just let it work.   it...

...strength,

...inner peace,

...what is to come.

...your frequency,

...the *flow,*

...flow with the outcome.

...the other side.

Clarity Gains

confusion reigns, so I must pray

confusion reigns; it must go, today

clarity gains

clarity gains

I sit still, opening myself to the sun

during these murky days

clarity gains

clarity gains

no more resistance

I calmly accept all that comes my way

courageously

I Dance for Her

I dance for   her

I dance for   her insecurities

                 her stress and anxiety

I dance for   patience, calmness, and to just breathe

I dance for   her past traumas, and toxic relationships

I dance for   her healing, for her spirit

I dance for   her confusion

                 not knowing which path she'd like to take

I dance for   her mistakes

                 her resilience and courage to drive through it all

I dance for   her lows, her highs

      for   her poetry lips, child-like laugh, and Gemini eyes

I dance for   her passionate heart, her loving soul

I dance for   her, for she is me

                 She deserves a limitless life

                 She deserves to be free, so

I dance

You Are Blessed!

don't get lost

in past thoughts

don't get caught

stuck, thinking of

everything that went wrong

you've been blessed!

see it

believe it

think it

The Breath

expand me
fill me
free me

remind me to be easy
travel through this journey lightly

we have convinced ourselves
we need wings to fly
when all we need is our mind
an imaginative mind
a strong body; breathe that circulates,
the blood that pumps within us,
urging us to keep going
to keep seeking our desires
to keep them fulfilled

I ask the breath -
the God-mind

to expand me
fill me
free me
remind me to tread lightly
and be easy

be   easy

My Plea to Society

turn up the love turn down the distractions

I want you to really see me
your eyes and your spirit have had enough
information overload from entertainment
pulled from social media platforms

put down your cell phone, look at me
no website is beyond the connection in front of you
living, breathing, human being here to exchange with you

no, we cannot go out to eat today
you're not really hungry
a hug is what you need

turn up the love, turn down the distractions
let's embrace, shift the focus
the dead receives too much of our praise
let's celebrate, rejoice in our alive

we are here, present
we can explore our relationships
with laughs, giggles, sweet memories
can we fill our spirit with this?

turn off the TV, turn up the radio
let's dance. Dance for love, for joy, for peace
dance for we are free
be present. Be here. let's be together

let's be.

Control

everyone
has a bubble

made of perception
and personal belief

to each his own
let go of control

within love, you find

there is no right
there is no wrong

let go of control
everything just is!

FOR: LOVE

Take Me to God

take me to the ocean

take me to the waterfalls

                    tell me you love me

                    with the right chakra

                    the heart chakra

let me dance with the moon

and make love to the sun

                    I've got to be one with God

                    I've got to feel God

                    take me to God

He, Me, & We

HE is water, fire, earth, & a whole lot of breath
into my soul
I can breathe again, I can see again
my senses are open to hear the wind again
I hear their prayers, I hear their thank you

HE is walking, talking nature
teaching ME to stand still, like the trees
showing ME the power of silence
to be like calm waves
back to peace again

HE speaks love-tied affirmations to my heart
sings lullabies & goodbyes to my wounds

HE firmly holds my hand, if I tumble into mistakes
HE is fully present with ME
happy & joyfully appreciative am I, with him
HE isn't worried about having his cake & eating it too
HE knows there's much more than cake
that can get you full

HE's addicted to the taste of my spiritual food
HE wants more of it on his plate & I lovingly feed him
HE gets spoonfuls of creativity
innovative ideas
child-like play

HE & I are laughter, jokes, & wisdom
Kisses, together

HE lingers on ME all day, everyday
& I linger on him all day, everyday
thank the heavens WE are awake
WE are ready for elevation
WE are change
WE are humble fame

Ase`

Living Water

living water, you are
I am living water
rushing through your memory
drowning your five senses
taking you deeper, much deeper
to those so called "untouchable fantasies"
now you're my reality.
You ready?....
I think you've been

I am aware and open
prepared for the coasting
because what we have
is rare and going extinct.
Sounds of serenity, like the ocean
bliss and wonders
let's implode from the waves of love
waves of love
pure truth, pure truth
me
you
truth
    truth
        truth…
cleanse the spirit
wash the soul of
all impurities
pure in our truth
pure in our moment
living water, we are.
Replenishing one another

cooling, cooling
the imprinted burns on our spirits
we're slowing down
in the gliding currents of the ocean
ocean
o c e a n
o c e a n

peace

you
me
love
cool
c o o l

Touch

on this warm day
I need soothing hands

fingers gliding
my shoulder blades

an exchange of love

waves of excitement
in the pit of my stomach

how I miss the touch
how I miss the love

the power of becoming one
I'll stay close to my daydreams

for this, I shall see
once again

Express

expressions
ex*pressions*

let me express my obsession
with this blissful energy we call love

I am just so intrigued, even fascinated
by the way it touches me
feels me
sees me
and heals me

it does backflips and somersaults
throughout my body
imagine what it does to my soul

my spirit must move faster
than the toddler
who just saw his mother
walk through the front door

oh love, I love what you do to me!
I love how you move me
how much care, compassion, creation, and counsel
you give me

since I know your power and how it fills me
I anticipate the moment I meet my love
to dwell in this feeling with another
who is honored by our commitment

oh love! how I adore ALL your intriguing feelings

From Waterfalls to Sunsets

From waterfalls to sunsets
The emotions. The energy. The change.

Rain droplets splurge
after storms cross our faces,
then sun blazes surge.

Erasing traces of any hectic weather,
we are warm again.

Like a rebirth, the water breaks,
a newborn emerges from a cozy womb.

What a cycle!

Flood of intensity,
streams of light
in your eyes

The emotions. The change.
From waterfalls to sunsets

We drown, we rise again, again

The feelings. The passion.
From waterfalls to sunsets

Life turns, everlasting

It is beautiful. It is precious.

Each season
From waterfalls to sunsets

Lessons and blessings

We see. We feel. We are.
From waterfalls to sunsets

We are.
From waterfalls to sunsets

Love Just *Is*!

love does not love, people do
she does not keep up with your faults
doesn't give a damn about
where you've been or what you did
she's not here to clock your every move
no, her job is to move you

she bares the bliss that dances
upon this Earth, this Universe
she reveals unexpected, unexplainable moments
Miracles

she could never blind you, stifle you
yet, she is called pain
love ain't ever caused me any pain
Expectations, Assumptions, Judgments
have

love never slips
she stands erect by my side
she whispers: "people come, go
they change
Let it go
I birth you; dwell within you"

she tells me to take her hand
let her fill me up
from my precious crown
to bottom of my soles
planted on the ground
she says don't wait
and I open myself to her

she is the only one
that can rattle the chaos out of my heart
clear my being of low vibes
replenish me with light
yet, they have looked in my eyes and said:

Love is pain
Love is blind

NO, their perception of her is clouded
she is the ultimate healer, quicker than time
let her caress and cradle your spirit

Call her
stop cursing her name
allow her to enchant your mental and emotional space
with peace, patience, compassion, beauty

love, oh love

they really don't know you
they misinterpret you
Free them, Release them
Unchain them

make them never let go of you again

Love is Love
Love is Love
Love is Love

Glide

talk about love...

we spiral into all night
I don't know what it is
deeper than love
what we do

I swear we were married in another lifetime

this connection is beyond strong
I'm addicted to the feeling of you on me
just touching, caressing, all day long
what did we do to each other?

some time ago, we created a deep bond

but now
now, I'm here trying to find another
because in this life we are not for each other
that's why we love and bump heads

hate and bump beds
make the sheets cry
and the walls scream
both our names

until we, off on each other's, came
drifting to a midnight's dream
but this, "let's sex and not be together"
just isn't me

this conflict of paths, of dreams
was frustrating. That's why I left
I came into what is truly for me
a new partner, a new reality

and I've dreamt of him
holding my hand tight
treating me as queen
all praises to the universe

all my hopes and dreams in this verse

I watched him from afar as I wandered in the holy land
eyeing the most beautiful shrine, he gleamed at me
had me laughing, cheeks burned

we came to be from lessons,
I finally learned how to let go

I thank you, all the love, all the hate, all the mistakes
brought me to the one, my ultimate love
who knew that after misery
you could meet a connection's infinity?

my partner, my peace

I found you
I found me

yeah, I found me

and together we glide
through the rest of these lifetimes

we glide, we glide, we *glide*

Like Water

when I look at you
I see something so chill and cool
like water

I could only imagine your rivers running
smooth and sweet
between green pastures
that lie beside you

much of what you do just flows through my mind

I could only imagine how deep your oceans are
and yes, I know you're not always calm

I know you have rushing waves
that crash against the beach of your chest
when you are troubled

see, I believe
I can bring your waves
back to their peace

I could only imagine
how it feels to be inside your lake
I want to swim in it

you are like water
you stay wet
I'll take your warmth, your cold

I want you to trickle on me
let go; pour your bliss into me
I want you to see yourself drip on me
I want to dive into you
surround all of me

don't worry about me dropping you
I don't want you to spill

you're much more beautiful, more powerful
when you're all together
I want to hear your sounds
I know they'll be heavenly

soft moans like the light crashing of a midnight sea

I want to be with you
there's something about your internal presence
that has me in a trance

visions of deeply
connecting with you
invade my daydreams

I know you can replenish me
you can fill me
you are healing

rejuvenating after life's intensities
you are like water; I need a drink

I need you to be part of the reason my hearts beats
I want you to be for me

I'll keep looking at you
there's something about you

so down to Earth, so intense
so captivating, so passionate

like water

I've Known Him

my soul knows him
he does not have to introduce himself

his energy has spoken
it's familiar

my heart speaks
his language

he is famous for being
the only man

with whom I've been
my absolute

complete
self

In loving memory:

ALANYA

An Angel passed by named Alanya

> Melanated wings, delicate like a baby's embrace, the strength was in her sincerity

Love, trust, behind laughter and a smile that sparkled like a Blood diamond amidst the mud of grief

Avatar, of God's devotion and empathy moving about touching our souls

Naked, vulnerable to earthly elements, in need of mankind's honest embrace

Yielding to divinity, feeling forsaken at times, not quite comprehending the evil, praying to inner-stand

At peace in the ethers, breath from the lungs of the Omnipotent God

> Yes, an Angel passed by

©2017 Darryl A. Lewis
All rights reserved.

The Author

I take heed as the universe speaks; clear, loud. I observe as it unfolds in front of me. With this new beginning, thankfulness comes to soul. As I keep moving, mind wide open, longing to pour out, lend me the paint brush.

I'll stroke a better me.

      Alanya (Painting Destiny)

www.ingramcontent.com/pod-product-compliance
Lightning Source LLC
Chambersburg PA
CBHW021001090426
42736CB00010B/1414